Focus on History

edited by Ray Mitchell and Geoffrey Middleton

Medieval Life

Viola Bailey and Ella Wise

Longman

The Middle Ages

From the Norman Conquest in 1066 to the present day is just over nine hundred years, or nine centuries. This can be shown in a diagram or Time Chart. The history you will study in this book belongs to part of the period of time known as the Middle Ages, or Medieval Times. It is shown by shading in the diagram below.

How can we learn about the lives of men and women who lived so long ago? The pictures in this book will show you some of the buildings, objects, maps, and writings, which have survived from the Middle Ages. From a careful study of these you will get a true picture of life in those days.

Wherever you live, you cannot be far from something belonging to the Middle Ages.

You may be able to visit museums, medieval churches, cathedrals, and castles.

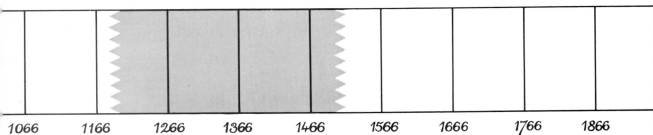

| 1066 | 1166 | 1266 | 1366 | 1466 | 1566 | 1666 | 1766 | 1866 |

Chepstow Castle, Monmouthshire,

For your work when you study this book, you will need a large
notebook. Print on the cover, 'MY DISCOVERY BOOK OF THE
MIDDLE AGES'. In this you can write stories, plays and notes
about your discoveries. At the back of your notebook, keep a list
of all the new words and their meanings. Head this page,
GLOSSARY.

Mark, on a blank map of Great Britain, all the towns, villages, and
districts you read about in this book.

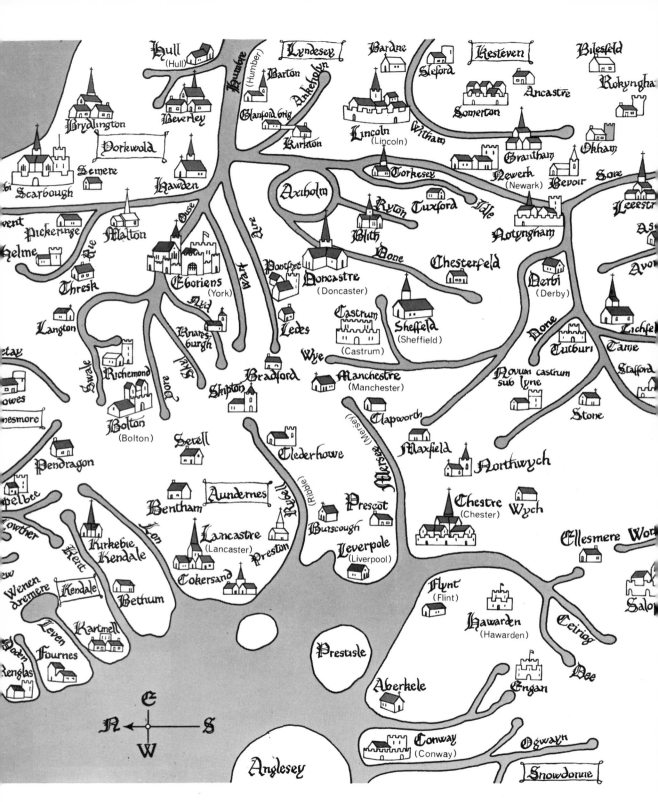

This is part of a fascinating map of Great Britain
drawn by an unknown artist about 600 years ago

4

Maps and Towns

This curious and ancient map was given to the Bodleian Library, Oxford, by a Mr Richard Gough. So it is called 'The Gough Map'.
Scholars think that the map was made for the use of travellers and Royal Messengers, or couriers.

On the map you will see that:
— spelling is often a little different from that of today.
— large towns show a church with a spire or a tower, a wall and some houses.
— towns of medium size have a church with a spire or a tower, one or two houses, but no wall.
— small towns are marked by a single building.
— the map is drawn with east and west where we put north and south.
— each river is shown rising in a kind of small lake. Look for the Rivers Mersey (Mersee), Ribble (Rybell), and Humber (Humbre).
— castles are drawn. Find Conway, Hawarden and Castrum.

Try to find on the map:
    Hull, Doncaster, Liverpool, Chester, Newark, Lancaster, Lincoln, Manchester, Bolton, Derby, Flint, Sheffield and York, marked as Eboriens.
In your notebook make a list of these towns.
Beside each town write the name again in medieval spelling, as shown on Gough's Map. Check if these towns were large, medium or small in medieval times.

Some parts of the Gough Map are worn and dirty. This is because hundreds of users have leaned on the map to study it.

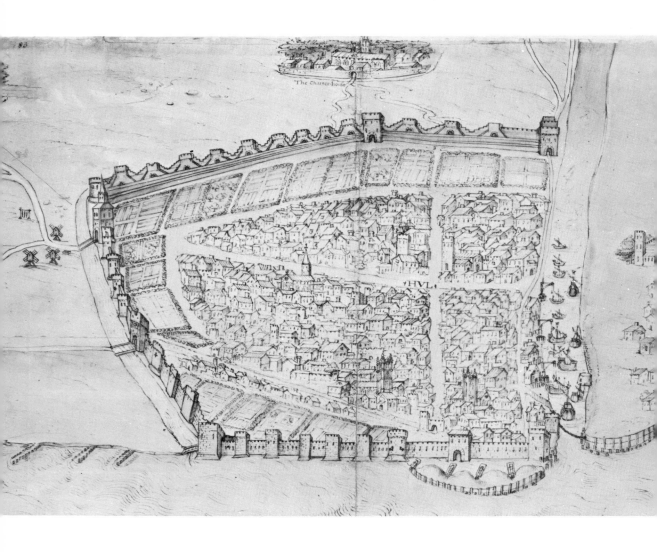

Here is a picture plan, drawn in the 14th century, of the walled town of Hull. You have seen Hull marked as a walled city on Gough's map. It was usual in the Middle Ages for towns to have walls round them for protection against enemies.

Hull was one of the first medieval cities to have fresh spring water carried by pipes to the town. It also had a home for old people called 'Le Maison Dieu', which is French for 'God's House'.

Search closely in the picture of Hull for:

  — the five gates in the walls.
  — the moat outside the walls.
  — the two cannon in one of the fortified towers.
  — the allotments inside the walls where fresh food was grown.
  — the six churches. The largest is the Church of Holy Trinity,
    where people still worship to-day.
  — the ships on the River Hull. How many can you see?
  — the wharves where ships are loading and unloading.
  — the derricks on the warehouses, for moving heavy cargoes. Hull
    traded with the Baltic, the Netherlands, and Bordeaux. Find these
    places on a map of Europe.
  — the fort near the mouth of the River Hull.
  — the chain across the mouth of the River Hull where it flows into
    the great River Humber. Can you guess why it was there?
  — the houses packed tightly together inside the walls.

Are there chimneys on all the houses? Many houses still had only clay-lined
holes for fireplaces. Wood was their main fuel. The large houses with
chimneys and fireplaces might burn the new 'Seacole'. This coal was brought
by sea from Newcastle.

Ships brought into Hull, wine, spices, pitch, iron, timber, furs, fruit, coal, tapestries, tallow, (animal fat used for soap and candles), and flax, (a plant from which linen is made).

Now you are ready to make your own picture plan of Hull.
The 'key' at the bottom of this page will help you.

Draw the walls and mark the gates.
Draw a fortified tower. Don't forget the cannon!
Show the moat and the drawbridges.
Draw the gardens under the walls.
Draw double lines to mark the main street.
Mark the warehouses.
Show the position of each church in red.
Draw the River Hull and name it.
Show the chain and fort on the River Hull.
Name the River Humber.

In your notebook, opposite your plan, write what you have learned
about medieval Hull.

Remember to draw a key like
this beneath your plan.

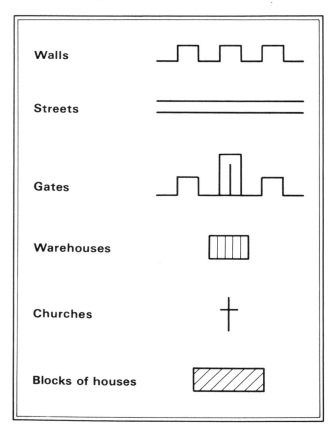

Securing the City

Here you see one of the gates of another walled city, Southampton. This gate still stands to-day. Look for the slots through which the defenders shot their arrows.

Through this gate passed knights and archers to take ship for France. They went to fight the French in some of the battles of the Hundred Years' War, which began in 1337.

We read from the Statutue of Winchester, that —
'The King hath commanded that in greate townes beinge walled, the gates shalbe closed from the sonne (sun) resting until the sonne rysing . . . and in every citie 6 men shall kepe at every gate . . . and shall watch the town al night.'
In your notebook first copy the King's command shown above, then rewrite the passage in modern English.

Do you know any towns where the streets have names like these: Eastgate, Westgate, Northgate, Watergate, Lowgate, Bargate, Newgate, Fishergate, Bridgegate, Foregate, Southgate and Monkgate? Each of these streets may have led to a gate in the wall of a medieval town.

Shops

Each medieval town had its shops. The 'shop' was usually the main room of the trader's house. Goods for sale were arranged on stalls.

Men of the same trade or craft often lived in the same street. What do you think was made or sold in: Tanners' Row, Bread Street, Rope Walk, Fish Lane, and Cornhill? Make a list of any streets with names like these in your town or village.

It was usual for a sign showing each man's trade or craft to hang above his shop. This was important because many people could not read. Try to find, from books in your library, pictures of such signs.

Now work in a group to make, from balsa wood and cardboard, models of shops. Make clay models of fish, meat, bread and other goods.

A Baker's Shop

A Fishmonger's Shop

For a tanner's shop cut out skins from small pieces of leather. Make miniature bales of cloth. Model, in clay, shop keepers and customers. Make and hang the shop signs on long poles.

Arrange your shops to make an exhibition for your classroom.

In this picture of a 15th century 'Woman's Shop',
how many . . . 'Merours . . . large and brode, and for
the syght, wonder gode' can you see?

Notice the jars of cosmetics, the two combs, the
customer's purse, the hair curlers and the lady's
hair!

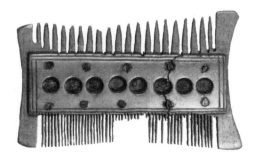

This medieval comb was one of the
treasures found during excavations in
London. It was made of bone and
bronze plates fastened with ten bone
pegs. Compare it with the combs on the
counter of the shop.

Markets and Fairs

In medieval times, weekly markets and yearly fairs were held by permission of the King. At the market goods made and grown in the district were sold. To the great fairs came traders from other towns and from foreign lands. These men brought strange and beautiful goods like —

jewellery, mirrors, swords, muslins, silks, and tapestries, perfume, spices, sugar, Mediterranean fruits and wines.

You will be interested to learn the cost of some 15th century goods:

Spectacles	20d	4 lbs sugar	4s 0d
I Purse of Yhalowe leder	1d	1 chicken	2d
Poyntels for writing	4d	10 eggs	1d
I ream spendable paper	8d	1 doz. white nightcaps	2s 3d
(wrapping paper)		(for use see page 47)	

A fair wage was 6d a day, so you will see that a pair of spectacles cost more than three days' pay, and one pound of sugar (a luxury), two days' pay. A modern workman may earn 100 sixpences a day. If he, like the medieval workman, had to work two days to pay for one pound of sugar, what would the sugar cost? Try to work out the value of other goods in this way.

Besides the buying and selling, fairs brought much fun and excitement. There were acrobats, wrestling, archery and performing animals like the horse in the picture.

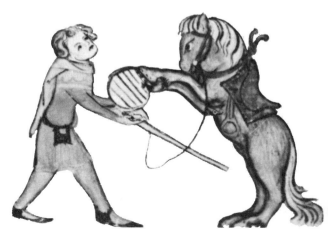

Puppet Shows like this were seen at fairs. Sometimes too there were miracle plays to watch. These were about Bible stories and were acted with much enjoyment. You may have seen the Chester Miracle Play, called 'Noyes Fludde', set to music by Benjamin Britten.

EAST ANGLIAN DAILY TIMES, SATURDAY, NOVEMBER 12, 1966

Lammas fair will not take place next year

COGGESHALL'S famous Lammas Fair — a revival of a mediaeval celebration — will not take place next year.

The fair is a revival of a mediaeval celebration. In 1250 the Abbot of Coggeshall, in his capacity of Lord of the Manor, was granted a charter to hold an annual fair, lasting eight days.

The fair has been revived in recent years, all profits going to charities.

What can you learn from this cutting from a newspaper? Find the meaning of the word LAMMAS.

Now head a page in your notebook: THE FAIR COMES TO COGGESHALL.

Imagine you were going to Coggeshall Fair six hundred years ago. Describe:

1 Your excitement.
2 What you saw on arrival.
3 The amusements.
4 The goods on the stalls.
5 The foreign traders.
6 What you bought at the Fair.

13

Breaking the Law

At every Fair, there was a 'Court of Piepowder', or 'pieds poudres', or 'dusty feet'. It was so called because men went straight in, dusty from the fair, to have their complaints settled on the spot.

The records of all Courts of Law were written, not in books but on parchment. You see here pieces of parchment sewn together to make a roll for a Coroner's Court. (A Coroner holds an inquest, or inquiry, on cases of sudden death.)

This paragraph was taken from a Coroner's Roll of London of the 14th century.

A Coroner's Roll from the Ipswich and East Suffolk Record Office

'At the hour of vespers . . . William struck with his hand a certain Johanna . . . and seeing this John Walsham, a tailor, being moved to anger drew his knife and mortally struck William. A certain Adam raised the 'Cry' . . . John fled to the Church of St. Edmund.'

Adam raised the 'CRY', or the 'HUE AND CRY'. All who heard it were expected to run and catch the criminal. Apprentices loved the chase; it was a break from long hours of work.

John was not caught however. He grasped the large ring knocker on the church door and called for 'Sanctuary', or refuge.

Every church had a right of 'Sanctuary', and could give shelter to a fugitive for a certain time, usually 40 days. After that time, he must either escape and become an outlaw, or agree to leave the country.

You know many stories of the famous medieval outlaw, Robin Hood. Imagine that John became an outlaw and joined Robin Hood's band.
Make a picture strip story of one of their adventures.

Knocker on the door of Aldham Church, Essex.

Find out if there is a fine knocker, like the one in the picture, on the door of any Parish Church in your district.

If John had been caught before he reached the Church, he might have been hanged on gallows like these.

Try to find out where gallows stood in your county. Look for names like:

> Gallows Hill,
> Gallows Corner,
> Gallows Grove,
> Gallows Field.

If you visited Westminster Abbey in London, you would find on the floor, in Poets' Corner, this inscription cut in the worn stone:

ROBERT HAWLE: KNIGHT

Murdered in the Choir

August II . 1378 .

Robert Hawle was chased round the Choir by fifty armed men, and killed in front of a terrified congregation. This was one occasion when the right of Sanctuary was broken.

Merchants

Every medieval town had its merchants. Robert Pagge was a merchant of Cirencester. In the Parish Church there is this memorial to him. It is a full-length portrait cut in brass.

If you study the Brass, you will see:
— the long, warm, fur-lined garment, called a Houppelande. It was fashionable from 1380 to 1450.
— the 'bagpipe' sleeves fashionable from 1405 to 1430.
— the pleats tacked down at the waist, fashionable from 1425 to 1450.
Between which years was the garment made?

Notice that the feet are resting on a sack of wool, or a 'woolsack'. What does this tell us about his trade? Look for the 'Merchant Mark' on the shield of the woolsack. Each merchant had his own mark. This was stamped on all his goods.

We read at Worcester in the fourteenth century:
'every bakere hab hys seal y-knowe upon his loff.'
What was the reason for this?
Do you know any bread to-day with a mark or a name stamped on the loaf?

17

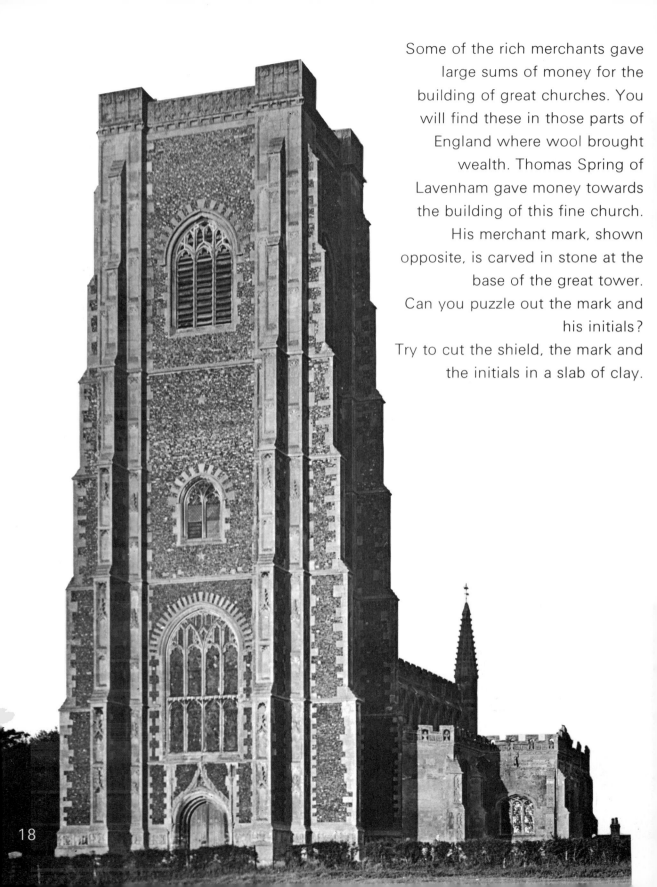

Some of the rich merchants gave large sums of money for the building of great churches. You will find these in those parts of England where wool brought wealth. Thomas Spring of Lavenham gave money towards the building of this fine church. His merchant mark, shown opposite, is carved in stone at the base of the great tower.
Can you puzzle out the mark and his initials?
Try to cut the shield, the mark and the initials in a slab of clay.

18

This fine signet ring is in the Guildhall Museum, London. The owner had his initials T.G. engraved on his ring. He pressed this into warm wax:
— to close his folded letters, as envelopes were not used at that time.
— to mark his business documents.
Make a potato cut of the merchant mark as you see it on this ring, and stamp it in your notebook.

Copy the merchant marks you find in this book, and write sentences about them.

Search in Parish Churches for merchant marks carved in stone and shown on brasses, on monuments, and in glass in windows. Keep a record of any you find.

Draw some merchant marks 9″ high and $\frac{1}{2}$″ wide, on Fablon or coloured plastic. Cut them out and press them on a window to make your own exhibition.

Special marks are still used by traders to-day, like the modern Woolmark and the Shell Mex mark. Make a collection of these trademarks from newspapers and magazines. Paste them in your notebook opposite the page of medieval merchant marks. Write across the top of these two pages:
MERCHANT MARKS OLD AND NEW.

19

The Wool and Cloth Trade

The picture below of sheep-shearing is shown on a
15th century manuscript. If you look carefully, you
will see:

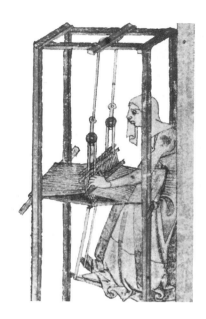

— the sheep ready for shearing,
— the cloth to keep the wool clean and to collect
  the pieces,
— the tool the 'Clipper' is using, (do we use such a
  tool to-day?)
— the shepherd in the background.

Here is the very beginning of the great wool and
cloth trade for which England was famous in the
Middle Ages.

Everyday clothing was made from wool. Spinning and weaving plain cloth for
the family was usually carried out in the home.
Wool for sale was collected, loaded, and carried away on strong packhorses.

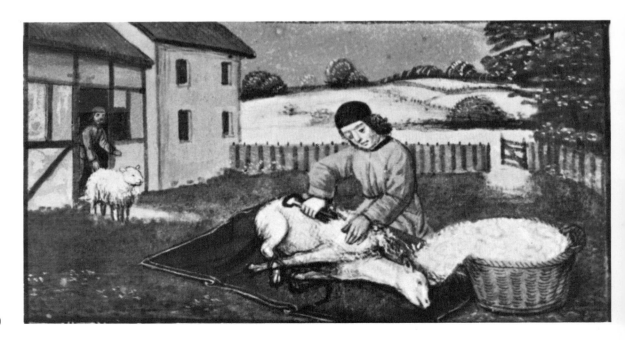

This picture shows you a string of packhorses
entering a town. They are loaded with woolpacks,
each weighing 240 lbs.
You may still find, in some parts of Britain,
packhorse bridges, like the one in the picture below
at Moulton Newmarket.
Sometimes the packhorse train rested for the night
at inns with names like these:

The Woolpack, The Drover, The Ram, The
Packhorse, and The Golden Fleece.
Make paintings of signs for two of these inns.

Look in your own town, or when you are on
holiday, for these and other inn signs connected
with the wool trade.

In your notebook, list them under these headings:

INN   STREET   TOWN

The best of English wool was sold to Flanders and Italy. There skilled weavers made it into fine cloth. Flanders was part of Belgium, Holland, and Northern France. Search for these on a map of Europe.

By order of the King, wool, hides, leather, lead and tin might be sold to foreign merchants only in certain English towns. These were called Staple Towns. Customs' officers in each Staple Town inspected the wool and collected a tax, usually 7/6d on each sack. The great sacks of wool for export weighed 26 stone. Merchants paid from £2 10s to £18 per sack.
When the English learned to make fine cloth, they began to sell this abroad.

A medieval clothier named Sherman lived at Dedham, Essex. The picture below shows you part of his home, warehouses, and office. It is still a home to-day.

Many people earned a living from wool.
There were Shepherds, Clippers, Woolpackers, Woolcombers, Spinners, Weavers, Shearmen, Fullers, Dyers, Tailors and Merchants.
Use a dictionary or encyclopaedia to find out what work each of these did.
You will find some explained under the word 'Wool'.

Look in the picture for the woman milking the sheep. Sheep were valued for:

— wool and leather,   — tallow for candles,
— cheese made from ewe's milk,   — meat for food,
— parchment for writing on,   — manure for the land.

Here is a business document written by a wool merchant. You will understand
it better if you read it aloud. Here are words to help you:

    bogwyt   = bought.   Norlache = Northleach.
    Cottyswolde = Cotswold.   refus   = refuse (waste).

'Item the XXIIII day of November I have bogwyt of Wyllyam Medewynter of
Norlache XI sacks of good Cottyswolde woll and medell woll . . . the pryse
the sacke of both good woll and medell woll XII marks . . . the refus woll to be
caste to Wyllyam Medewynter the woll packer.'
There was no English coin for a mark, but its value was reckoned at 13/4d.

In your notebook, under the title, 'The Wool Trade',
write paragraphs on:

1 Sheepshearing   3 Transport of Wool
2 Workers in the Wool Trade 4 Products from Sheep
Illustrate your work where possible.

Merchants' Homes

Merchants who grew rich built themselves fine houses. Below is the house of William Grevel of Chipping Campden in Gloucestershire. This beautiful house is still lived in to-day.

Find out from the picture:
— what materials were used for the walls,
— if the roof was thatched or tiled,
— where the sundial was placed,
— if 'al the windows' . . . were . . . 'wel y glased ful clere'. These words come from a poem by a famous medieval poet, Geoffrey Chaucer. Glass at this time was scarce and expensive.

The main room of the house had a fine fireplace. From letters and wills we learn about the furnishings. On the walls were hung tapestries or gay cloth hangings. The floors were made of oak boards or tiles.

This carved oak chest belonged to a medieval merchant. Can you
make out his name, N. FARES, carved on the front panel?
The chest was the main item of furniture in the medieval home.
Some chests were simple and others were beautifully carved.
A chest took the place of our safe, wardrobe, bookcase,
cupboard, desk, and chest of drawers. It was sometimes used for
a seat, a table, a travelling trunk, and even a bed.
Linen, documents, and valuables were stored in chests.

Every medieval church also had a chest. The
one in the picture below is from Milton
Bryant in Bedfordshire. If there is a chest in
your Parish Church, ask what was stored in it.
Then draw the chest and write a paragraph
about it.

The house of rest

In this simple living room, you see three pieces of furniture
— a bench, on which a man is sitting,
— a stool,
— a table made of boards resting on trestles.
These could be found in most homes by the end of the
Middle Ages. Study the picture carefully. Can you name
twelve other objects in this room?
A rich merchant would have in his house a solid oak table
with fixed ends instead of trestles. He would have his own
chair, like the one on page 30. There would be cushions
on the stools and benches to make them more comfortable.

When a man died he left his belongings to his family
and friends. A medieval architect, in his will, left to his
niece Jenete:
    'iiij (4) of the grene Kusshones . . . viij (8) dysshes
    iij (3) candelstykkes . . . and a long table.'

26

It may surprise you to know that this jug is over 600 years old. Decorated jugs of this shape are still made by potters today. When you see such a jug, draw it in your notebook. Then draw the medieval jug beside it. Write a sentence about each.

Pottery jugs were used for carrying wine and beer from casks to table. Find out why water was not a very popular drink nor indeed a very safe one in the Middle Ages.

Drinking cups could be made of horn, pewter or silver. This drinking cup, 5½'' high, of silver-gilt, was called a Mazer. Sometimes pet names were given to them. One owner called his drinking cup: Crumpledud. This name was marked on the cup. Such a mazer was sold recently for £10,000.

Just as you would find a saucepan in every modern kitchen, so this type of cooking pot would be found in every medieval home.
This pot, made of bronze, was found buried deep in the earth under a London street. It could be used standing on its three legs *in* the fire, or hanging from a hooked chain over it.

27

The strange object you see here is a medieval candlestick. As the legs fold, it could be used for travelling.

Find:
- the spike, or Pricket, which held the candle.
- the socket, for a candle or a Rushlight.
- the hinges on the legs.

The best candles were made of beeswax. Cheap candles were made by dipping wicks into melted fat. After cooling, these were dipped and cooled again. This was repeated until the candles were of the right thickness.

Rushes, collected near streams, were peeled to the last two layers. They were then dried and dipped to give a thin layer of tallow. A rushlight two feet long would burn for about an hour.

Candles are still in use to-day. Sketch a medieval and a modern candlestick and write sentences about each.

A medieval brass candlestick found in London

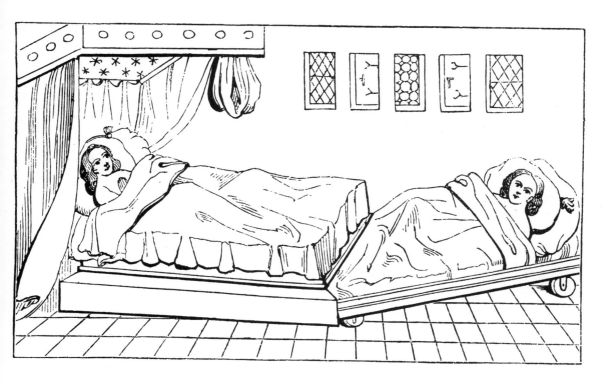

What can you learn from a close look at this medieval bedroom?
Take a little time over this.

Have you missed any of these details:
— the canopy and curtains to keep the sleepers snug and warm?
— the Truckle bed? This was made to be stored under the larger bed. Notice
   the wheels. A child or a servant might sleep in such a bed.
— the window-shutters with latches and hinges?
— the tiled floor?

A bed would have been very comfortable with 'a materas . . . a fether beed . . .
a great pilve (pillow) . . . a small pilve . . . blankets . . . good shetes . . . a
coverlete . . .' as we read from the will of John Baret of Bury, who died
in 1463.

Follow the directions on this page, and make a model stage to show the merchant in the main room of his house.

1 Stand a strong cardboard box, without a lid, on its long side.

2 On the back wall, draw windows and a door as in the house on page 24.

3 Paint a fireplace on a side wall. There is a picture on page 26.

4 On the opposite wall fasten hangings of striped cloth.

5 Paint the floor to look like oak boards or tiles. A medieval tile is shown in the picture on the left.

6 Use balsa wood to make a chest, a table, a chair, and a bench and stools like the one below. You will find descriptions and pictures on this page and on pages 25 and 26.

7 Make small clay models of the jug and the mazer shown on page 27.

8 Draw and cut out in a suitable size, a cardboard model of the merchant on page 17. Stand him in a slot in a small block of balsa wood.

Now pretend you are the wool merchant. Some of your friends are foreign traders visiting your home. Tell them about your life and work. You can gather the facts you need from pages 17 to 29.

This woollen cap was found in Worship Street, London. In the rim was found hidden a gold quarter Noble of King Edward III.

(Look at the Noble on page 33.)

If you go to London, you should visit the Guildhall Museum, where this cap is kept with other interesting remains of the Middle Ages.

Look carefully at this picture of a merchant painted by Hans Holbein.

Notice that the cap he is wearing is like the cap found in London.

You can see that the merchant is breaking the seal on a folded letter.

Read again the paragraph at the top of page 19.

Money

Here you see a photograph of the Short Cross Silver Penny of King Henry II.
There were no halfpennies, so people cut along the short crosses to make halves and quarters of a penny. Some people cheated. They cut off small pieces of the coins beyond the ends of the crosses. These tiny pieces were saved up and sold.

King Henry III made a Long Cross Silver Penny like this to try to stop the thieving of silver.

In the reign of King Edward I, silver halfpennies and quarter pennies (farthings) were minted So there was no further need to cut the pennies into halves and quarters. This king also made the new silver coin pictured here. It was called a Groat, and was worth four pennies.

The coin you see here is called an Angel. If you look closely you will see the Archangel Michael standing on a dragon, and spearing it.
The Angel was minted in gold by King Edward IV. It was worth 6/8d, like the Noble, which is shown on the opposite page.

King Edward III had minted a beautiful gold coin called a Noble to celebrate a great victory. The English navy had defeated the French at the Battle of Sluys off the coast of Flanders, in 1340.
This picture shows the coin twice its real size.

On the Noble, look for the king in his ship and find his shield. On this is shown his Royal Coat of Arms. In the four quarters of the shield you will see the lilies for France and the lions for England.
The box-like parts fore and aft on the ship were called 'castles'. Why were they there? The word 'castle' should give you a clue. The name 'fore-castle' or 'fo'c'sle' is still used today.

In 1966 a boy aged five found four gold coins at Fishpool near Mansfield, Nottingham. These were part of a great hoard of 1,236 gold nobles which were hidden in 1464. To-day each noble is worth £41.
If you are lucky enough to find treasure in gold or silver, you must declare it to the police. When the value has been judged, you will be given the money payment due to you.

Schools & Colleges

In this schoolroom the master holds a birch rod. Can you guess why? Search in the picture for at least six things which are different from those in your classroom. Towards the end of the Middle Ages, most towns had grammar schools. A rich merchant's son would attend one of these schools. The school day was 8 hours long. Boys were taught some simple mathematics, and to speak, to read, and to write in Latin. This was the language of scholars everywhere in Europe. Find out if there are, in your district, any grammar schools which were started in the Middle Ages. In your notebook, draw the badges and write the mottoes of these schools. Books were very scarce and precious, and some were chained to the bookcases as in this library at Hereford Cathedral.

At 15 years of age a boy could study at one of the new Colleges at Oxford or Cambridge. This picture shows a corner of the medieval building of Merton College, Oxford. Read aloud the paragraph below describing the life of some students at a college in Cambridge.

'There be students whych ryse dayly betwixte foure and five and from five untyll sixe use prayer . . . and from sixe unto ten use pryvate study or lectures. At ten they go to dynner wyth a penye pyce (piece) of byefe (beef) with otemell (oatmeal) and nothynge els. After thys slender dynner they be learnynge untyll five when they have supper not much better than their dyner. After, they go on to some studye untyll nyne or tenne; and being wythout fyre runne up and downe halfe an hour to gette a heate on their feete when they go to bed.'

Imagine you are one of the students. Write a letter to your father telling him of your life at Cambridge. Begin your letter: Right Worshipful Sir, because fathers were very strict in training their sons, and there were harsh punishments for disobedience. End your letter: From your obedient son, and add your name.

Medicine

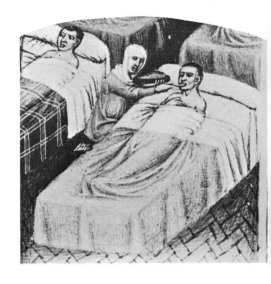

On these two pages are pictures taken from medieval manuscripts. Ask yourself, in each case, what is the matter with the patient? Is any treatment being given? What do you think of the hospital beds? How are they different from those in a modern hospital?

Here is a medieval prescription for a simple anaesthetic, which was used to try to stop people feeling pain.

> 'The seed of henbane . . . in wyne to drynk maketh the drynker . . . for to slepe, that he schal noght fele whatsoever is done to hym.'

Henbane is a plant still used in medicine to-day.

There was, however, little that could be done to ease very severe pain, or to cure disease. Sometimes there were terrible plagues. One of these was called the Black Death. Read about this in other history books.

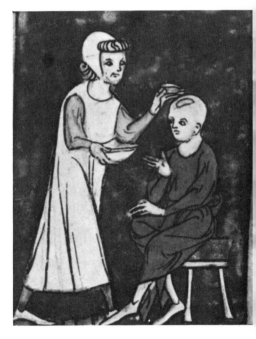

A few students at the Universities of Oxford and Cambridge studied to become doctors. Much that they learned came from a famous medical school at Salerno in Italy.

Help for the sick and injured was also given by the monks and nuns. They used herbs from the monastery gardens for medicines.

In the villages many remedies were made from plants, insects and animals. Here are two prescriptions from those days:

'To cure a chest complaint . . . use butter, oil of sweet almonds, marsh mallow root, or oil of violets; make an ointment and anoint the chest therewith.'

'Cut off the heads and wings of . . . crickets and put them with beetles and common oil into a pot . . . leave a day and a night in a bread oven . . . pound the whole and rub the sick parts.'

You can now try to write a diary for a day in the life of a doctor in the Middle Ages. Remember to include treatment and prescriptions.

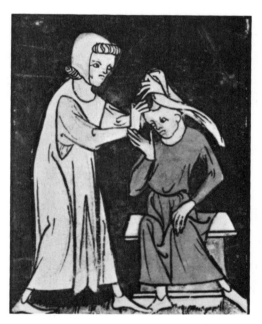

Games and Pastimes

We know from manuscripts that, in the Middle Ages, boys and girls and their parents enjoyed games as much as they do to-day. The pictures you see on these pages are taken from a manuscript in the Bodleian Library, Oxford.

In this picture notice how the boys fixed the rope for the swing.

Look at the game of chess. Do we still use a board exactly like this?

You see in this picture that the boys are interested in imitating a sport enjoyed by knights. What is it called? Can you think of any game played by children to-day which has taken the place of this medieval game?

In the description below you should be able to recognise another sport enjoyed in the Middle Ages:

'When the great marsh . . . is frozen, throngs of youths . . . fit to their feet the shin bones of beasts, lashing them beneath their ankles, and with iron shod poles in their hands . . . are borne along swift as a bird.'

Other sports and pastimes enjoyed were: Whip and Top, Hoops, Football, Hockey, Cricket, Kayles (Pin Bowling), Cards, Dancing, Wrestling, Hunting and Hawking. In the picture below, the children are playing Oranges and Lemons. Search in other history books for pictures of any games. Study all the pictures carefully and notice costumes, hair styles and footwear.

With the help of your friends, make paintings for a frieze for your classroom wall, with the title: Games and Pastimes in the Middle Ages.

There came a time when men were forbidden to play games. Skilled archers were needed for the wars against France. The King ordered that:
'Throughout the realm of England, no man should use any play or pastime save only the longbow and arrows, on pain of death.'

Do you think the men in the picture above are enjoying this new law?
Each had two arrows for practice. Guess who scored a 'Bull's Eye'?
Which man shot wildly?

Did you know that:
— a leather strap called a Bracer was worn on the left wrist? This protected the wrist when the bowstring twanged back after shooting.
— the longbow was as tall as a man?
— each arrow was a yard long? It was steel-tipped to pierce armour.
— barbed arrows were used for hunting?
— the left shoulder and straight left arm pointed to the target?
— the end of the arrow shaft was drawn back to the right ear?
— a good archer could fire twelve arrows a minute and send them 250 yards?

Write a paragraph about Archery and illustrate it with a cut-out picture of an archer with a longbow.

Building

A medieval plane

Have you ever visited any of these great cathedrals: Wells, York, Chester, Winchester, Durham, Exeter, Lincoln, Peterborough, Norwich, Worcester, Ely, Hereford, Salisbury, St. Albans, Gloucester, Lichfield, Ripon, Bristol, St. Giles (Edinburgh), Canterbury, or Westminster Abbey in London?
They show the remarkable work of the master craftsmen of the Middle Ages. In the picture below you see some of these craftsmen at work. A mason, wearing a high hat, is shaping a block of stone. What tool is he using? How is the workman mixing the mortar? Notice his strong boots. What is the tool being used by the workman on the middle tower?
Have you ever wondered how workmen raised heavy loads before the invention of power machinery?
In the picture they have a clever device of wheel and pulley to hoist the heavy buckets. This method is sometimes used to-day.

Armour

This is a picture of Canterbury Cathedral, built by medieval craftsmen. In this cathedral there is the tomb and copper-gilt figure, or effigy, of Edward, the Black Prince, who died in 1376.

On the opposite page you can see the slim, graceful armour in which the Black Prince fought his battles. More than twenty pieces were specially beaten into shape to make a perfect suit for him.

Remember a knight had to be able to move in armour. Look at the effigy to see the clever use of:

— chain armour (called Mail) under the arms and round the neck so that he could move his arms and head.

— the overlapping metal plates on his shoes, shoulders and gauntlets.

Compare these with the shell of a lobster, which is arranged in a similar way so that it can move more easily.

Look at the effigy of the Black Prince and find:

1 the egg-shaped close-fitting helmet. Round it is the Prince's coronet.
2 the arm plates in three parts:
   a) from wrist to elbow,
   b) from elbow to shoulder,
   c) the elbow guards.
3 the gloves or gauntlets, with knuckledusters called GADLINGS.
4 the plates called CUISSES strapped on the front of the thighs over his leather breeches.
5 the shin plates called GREAVES.
6 the knee pieces.
7 the metal shoes called SOLLERETS.
8 the horizontal sword belt worn on the hips. This became fashionable during the lifetime of the Black Prince.
9 the long-hilted sword.

The Black Prince also wore ROWEL SPURS as shown in this picture.

If you look again at the effigy of the Black Prince, you will see that he wears over his body armour a tight-fitting tunic called a JUPON. On this and on his shield you see the Royal Coat of Arms, showing the lilies for France and the lions for England.

Right across the top of both the Jupon and the Shield is a mark like a large letter 'E'. This is called a LABEL. The eldest son always wears a Label over his family coat of arms.

If you visit the Tower of London, be sure to look for the Black Prince's Ruby among the Crown Jewels. It was given to him by Pedro the Cruel of Castile (Spain). Pedro was to have married the Black Prince's sister but she died on her way to the wedding.

Read, from other history books, more about the Black Prince and his exciting life.

Make an interesting booklet about him, with illustrations. Trace or draw an outline of his effigy, mark in the armour and label it.

ICH DIEN

Make and paint a clay model of the effigy. Mix a gold colour for the armour. Paint the lilies gold on a blue background, and the lions gold on a red background.

Badges & Pilgrimages

Do you recognise this badge? We are told it belonged to the blind King John of Bohemia who was killed at the Battle of Crecy in 1346.

The Black Prince found the badge on the battlefield, and it has been the personal badge of each Prince of Wales since that time. Find on the badge the motto, 'ICH DIEN', which means 'I Serve'.

Do you collect badges? On this page you see badges collected by pilgrims from sacred places called SHRINES. Look for the badges of pilgrims if you visit the London Museum and the Guildhall Museum. People went on pilgrimages for special reasons:
— to be healed.
— to ask forgiveness for their sins.
— to seek help when they were in trouble.
— to give thanks.

Pilgrimages were very popular; they were like organised tours and holidays. The shrine of Saint Thomas Becket in Canterbury Cathedral brought thousands of pilgrims from this country and abroad. Thomas Becket was an Archbishop of Canterbury. He was murdered by four knights in the cathedral on a winter's evening in 1170. Ask at the library for a book from which you can read the story of Thomas Becket.

45

One pilgrimage is described in a long poem called 'The Canterbury Tales', written by Geoffrey Chaucer. He was about thirty-six years old when the Black Prince died.

The pictures on this page are taken from a beautiful manuscript of the poem. They show Chaucer and two of the thirty pilgrims.

This young Squire, the son of a Knight, was one of the pilgrims. Chaucer writes of him:

'He was as fresshe as is the monthe of May.

Short was his gowne with sleves long and wyde.

Wel koude he sitte on horse and faire ryde.'

Here is another of the pilgrims, the 'Wife of Bath'. She had been on many pilgrimages. In Chaucer's words, she was:

'A worthy woman al hir lyfe.

And thries hadde she been at Jerusalem,

At Rome she hadde been and at Boloigne.'

Even though Chaucer's spelling is very different from ours, you will understand his meaning if you read his words aloud.

46

From the picture, what can you learn about a medieval inn?

Look first at the guests arriving. How are they dressed for travelling?

Find the inn sign. Can you guess the name of the inn?

Are there any sheets, bedcovers, and pillows on the beds? What is on the stool? Why have so many beds been placed in this room?

Do you think this is a good clean inn?

Do you live near, or know of, any place of medieval pilgrimage? There were many including Holywell, Walsingham, St. David's, St. Edmundsbury, and Glastonbury. Did you know that pilgrimages are still made to-day to Mecca in Saudi Arabia, and to Lourdes in France? You can find information about these and other pilgrimages in Volumes 1 and 3 of the Oxford Junior Encyclopaedia.

Now prepare a 'Leaflet for Tourists', giving simple facts about one place of pilgrimage, medieval or modern. Draw your favourite Pilgrim's Badge on the cover, under the title.

Index

Amusements 12, 13
Archery 40
Armour 42—44

Badges 44—45
Becket, Thomas 45
Bedroom 29
Black Prince, The 42—45
Building 41

Canterbury Tales, The 46
Cathedrals 41—42
Chained Books 34
Chaucer Geoffrey 24, 46
Chests 25
City Gates 9
Coat of Arms 33, 44
Coggeshall Fair 13
Colleges 35
Coroner's Roll 14

Effigy 42—43

Fairs 12, 13
Furniture 25, 6, 29, 30

Gallows 16
Games and Pastimes 38—39
Gough's Map 4—5
Grevel's House 24

Houppelande 17
Household Goods 26—27,
    29, 30
Homes, Merchants' 22, 24
Hue and Cry 14
Hull 6—7, 8

Imports and Exports 7, 12,
    22
Inns 21, 47

Lighting 28
Longbow, The 40

Markets 12
Medicine 36—37
Merchant 17—19, 22—24,
    26, 31
Merchant Marks 17—19
Money 32—33

Packhorses 21
Pagge, Roberts 17
Pedro of Castile 44
Pie Powder Court 14
Pilgrimages 45—47
Plays 13
Prescriptions 36—37
Prices of Goods 12
Products from Sheep 23

Sanctuary 15—16
Schools 34
Shops 10—11
Shrines 45, 47
Spring, Thomas 18
Staple Towns 22

Treasure Hoard 33

Westminster Abbey 16, 41
Wills 26, 29
Wool Trade 18, 20—23